The Power Of S

How To Stop Beating Yourself Up, Take Action And Achieve Success In Your Life

By

Stuart Wallace

Table of Contents

Introduction 5
Chapter 1: What Is Positive Self-Talk? ..9
When And Where Is Self-Talk Helpful? 12
Chapter 2: You Are What You Think ...18
How Does Self-Talk Work? 20
Chapter 3: Consciously Rule Your Subconscious 29
What Positive Self-Talk Does For Your Brain.......30
Beating Negative Self-Talk Out Of Your Head......32
Create Self-Distance 33
Visualize 36
Set Smart Goals..37
The Benefits Of Mindfulness Meditation..............40
Neutralize Cognitive Distortions 42
Chapter 4: Self-Talk And Your Family 53
Self-Talk To Improve Relationships With Your Family 54
How To Avoid Taking Negativity Out On Family..61

Teach Your Children Positive Self-Talk 64
Transfer Positivity To Your Spouse........................68
Speak To Your Spouse Nicely 68
Focus On The Good Things 69
Listen Impersonally 70
Respect Boundaries And Needs 71
Repel Pessimism 73
Do Happy Things 73
Eliminate Jealousy And Insecurities 76

Chapter 5: Self-Talk For Business Success 78
Make Impossible Tasks Possible 79
Improve Your Interpersonal Relations 87
Gain Self-Motivation For Tedious Tasks 98

Chapter 6: Positive Self-Talk For Social Relations 109
Overcoming Shyness With Self-Talk....................110
Self-Talk For Better Communication 115
Self-Talk To Improve Self-Esteem 118

Chapter 7: Positive Self-Talk For Your Love Life 124

Grow Your Self-Esteem And Improve Your Body Image 125

Get Someone's Attention 128

Chapter 8: Growing Positive Self-Talk As A Habit 133

Power Of Positive Affirmations 134

Eliminate Procrastination 138

Conclusion 146

References 150

Disclaimer 157

Introduction

The endless loop of negative thinking plagues you from day to day. You feel that you can't do anything right and you believe that you are a horrible person. Sometimes, you wonder if there was a way to break through the negative self-talk and make yourself more successful.

You can stop wondering. There is indeed a great way to bring about success in all areas of your life. The way is positive self-talk.

I was raised in a negative environment. Hence, my mind was programmed to think negatively. I would beat myself up every chance I got, and I would hang back from success at work and in my love life by telling myself that I wasn't able to achieve my dreams. When I discovered positive self-talk in a CBT course, I thought, "Is there something significant here?" Building off of the course, I began to learn more about positive self-talk. Now I am married to the woman of my dreams, I have completed my graduate degree, and I have earned several promotions at work. All of my success centers around my new way of talking to myself.

Your life is built around the kind of thoughts you think. You inadvertently sabotage everything you want for yourself with negative thinking and self-doubt. By using positive self-talk, you can change your life around. From improving relationships with your family to earning a promotion at work to opening your own business, you can motivate yourself with positive self-talk. Success is not for the privileged few; it is for everyone who works for it. With a little concentrated work on your self-talk, you can make all of your dreams come true and break out of the cycle of negative self-talk that is holding you back.

This book is the solution to the negative self-talk that keeps you stuck in the same miserable state, day after day, year after year. You obviously want your life to change for the better, or you wouldn't be reading this book. Success can be yours when you apply the concepts in this book to your family, your love life, your social life, and your business or work.

I promise you that by the time you finish this book, you will know how to change your life around. You will be able to achieve everything you keep telling yourself is not possible. Motivation and success will be yours for the taking.

If you keep engaging in negative self-talk, you will continue to be unhappy. You will continue to be passed over for promotions or raises at work, you will continue to put your goals on hold, and you will continue to receive social and romantic rejections. Problems within your family, such as fighting, will also continue. But if you take action now, you can solve all of these problems and more.

Don't hesitate. Start working on your self-talk today and you will see enormous benefits. Read on to grow your self-esteem, become motivated, and reach new levels of success that you never imagined were possible. You can change your present state of negativity, but only if you start working on it now!

Chapter 1: What Is Positive Self-Talk?

What is this positive self-talk I keep speaking about? As you have probably noticed, you tend to talk to yourself. It's not crazy – everyone does it. A constant narrative runs in your mind, telling you what to do, informing you of who you are. The voice may sound like your own, or like someone else's, such as a parent or teacher you once had. The voice may change tone and message depending on your mood and situation.

This is your self-talk. It is your brain's way of directing your actions and processing the information you receive from the world around you in a way it can handle [1]. Your self-talk may be negative, in that you tell yourself bad things, call yourself names, or dwell on bad things that have happened to you. Or it could be positive, always uplifting you with encouraging words. Positive self-talk is obviously the better of the two forms of self-talk, as it motivates you to do your best and keeps your mood bright.

Now chances are, if you are reading this, you already have a profound familiarity with negative self-talk. It has probably plagued you for years. You tell yourself that you can't do things. You insult and berate yourself for every mistake. Constantly, you are in a bad mood because your mind tells you awful things. You know that this self-talk is toxic, yet you can't seem to change it.

The truth is that you *can* change your self-talk. Through some work, you can reprogram your mind to think more positively. I know this is possible because I did it myself. I won't lie and claim that changing your thinking is the easiest thing in the world, but I do know that you can make it happen through repetition and other techniques that I cover throughout this book. In addition, I know that the benefits are tremendous in all areas of life. Changing your self-talk from negative to positive is certainly worth the effort.

To start the process of motivating yourself and gaining success through positive self-talk, you need to make a goal now: "I will start talking to myself like I am my own best friend."

That is the essence of positive self-talk. You build yourself up, instead of tearing yourself down. You think thoughts centered around how great of a person you are and how you can handle any challenge that life throws at you. You treat yourself like a best friend, encouraging and pushing yourself through life's hardest moments and biggest struggles. When you feel bad, you lift yourself up and seek comfort in healthy activities.

Positive self-talk is not thinking happy thoughts all of the time. It is more than possible to criticize yourself and correct your mistakes or reflect on how bad a problem is at the present moment. However, you do these things in a way that makes you feel better. You focus on solutions, rather than problems, and you don't hurt your self-esteem by repeating hurtful observations or insults to yourself.

When And Where Is Self-Talk Helpful?

We all have areas of life that can benefit and flourish from positive self-talk. As you learn to use positive self-talk, you will notice that all areas of your life improve. This is because your self-talk influences your attitude, and your attitude influences your actions. Having a positive attitude will cause you to act in ways that bring greater rewards to you than a negative attitude.

The first and foremost place where positive self-talk brings about good change is within yourself. Your self-esteem and confidence will grow. You will suddenly have the self-love required to take big risks and mitigate the problems that may arise in life. Fear will melt away, replaced by a self-assurance that you can do anything you set your mind to. You will instantly start to feel better about who you are as a person, how you look, what you have done in the past, and how you will tackle your dreams.

This has a trickledown effect in every other aspect of your life. Your interpersonal relationships, such as your friendships and familial relationships, will suddenly improve. This is because you show the ones you love more positivity and you become pleasanter to be around. You also handle interpersonal conflicts more effectively because you are no longer plagued by insecurities. Issues like jealousy or taking things too personally will fade away because you have more self-esteem. Your positive attitude will make you a more patient parent, and you will teach your kids better life skills by modeling positive self-talk for them.

You will also have the confidence to build new relationships. You will no longer want to hang back in shyness because you believe that you are a likable person. Other people will enjoy getting to know you. Your social circle will grow.

You will enjoy a better love life and more dates if you are still single. You will finally have the self-esteem that others find more attractive, plus you will smile more. If you are already married, you will have more fun with your spouse and bring more friendships into your life. This will make you a better spouse. I was single and suffering from constant romantic rejections when I was stuck in the negative self-talk loop; I was often stood up! Then I began to believe in my worthiness and I was able to attract my wife. Now she and I have many friends and enjoy many activities outside of our home, separate and together. Having these activities and friends makes our marriage fun and exciting.

With improved social relations, you will open up more opportunities and fewer conflicts. You can find people who will help you succeed in life and make them want to work with you. Potential clients will find you more likable, and therefore you will make more money. My improved social skills and positive attitude have made it possible for me to form many lucrative work relationships.

This can drastically improve your work life and your performance. You will also have more confidence to attract new clients, tackle bigger projects, and take more calculated risks. Your boss will notice your heightened work ethic, and you can expect promotions or raises. Climbing up the corporate ladder starts with believing that you are destined for the top.

If you want to start your own business or go after a new job, you will have the confidence to do so. You know that you can achieve what you want in life. But you also know that if you are rejected by a potential job or if your business fails, you won't be failing at life. You can get back up from rejection and failure with less pain and you can learn from your mistakes in order to do better in the future. This self-assurance and self-love make you able to take on risks that can move your life forward. You are not really going after your dreams if you don't take some risks.

For instance, I took a big risk when I decided to leave a job I hated and start a freelance career. I didn't know if I would even be able to pay the bills with a freelance job, but I thought I might as well try. Before I started positive self-talk, I wanted to try freelancing but I kept telling myself that I would probably fail at it and end up bankrupt. After starting positive self-talk, I was able to convince myself that I had every skill necessary to make freelancing work. Then I started and I enjoyed far more success than I thought possible.

Eventually, I decided to make freelancing a side gig and went after a job with a Fortune 500 company. Again, I didn't think I could get it, but I assured myself that it would not hurt to try. My palms sweat and I trembled in my shoes in the lobby as I wanted to be taken in for my interview. Was my resume good enough? Was my freelance experience something that could be taken seriously? I kept reminding myself that I had what it took for the job and I was the best candidate out of all my competition. I was dressed for success and I had a smile plastered on my face. *I got this,* I kept telling myself.

Guess what? I got the job and I have received two promotions in two years. Was I fearless? Absolutely not. But I used positive self-talk to make something great out of that fear.

Chapter 2: You Are What You Think

Je pense, donc je suis. "I think, therefore I am." This phrase is famous because it is true. Our ability to reason and apply logic or emotion to situations makes us human.

But the reverse is also true: You are what you think. The thoughts that go through your mind define you and instruct your brain to view you in a certain light. Hence, changing your thoughts can change who you are.

You would not be who you are today if not for your self-talk. Now you must ask yourself: Am I happy the way I am? If you are depressed, fatigued, and lacking in confidence because of negative self-talk, you are not being your best self. You have so much potential that you bury underneath thoughts like, "I couldn't possibly do that" or "I don't have what it takes." You turn down great opportunities out of fear, you ignore great people because you don't think you're worthy of their friendship, and you drive people who love you away with your negativity and insecurities. That is not how you become successful and win at life.

When you change your internal dialogue from negative to positive, you also change the way you feel and act. You feel better, and thus you project positivity outward. This makes the world kinder to you.

I bet you know someone who always seems positive and upbeat. This person brightens the room when he or she walks in. This person also seems to get what he or she wants without too much effort. Things always work out for this person – even bad things tend to turn out positive in the end for him or her.

Instead of feeling jealous of this person, think about how you can be more like him or her. This enviable person simply has a positive mindset that unlocks doors for him or her in all areas of life. This person doesn't let negative thinking ruin everything. He or she also doesn't engage in comparisons and feel inadequate next to others. "I can do it" seems to be this person's mantra in life. By adopting a similar mindset and self-talk, you can certainly make yourself like this person, always attracting good things in life and radiating positivity.

Now let's consider the science behind why the energy of your self-talk makes such a huge difference in your quality of life.

How Does Self-Talk Work?

Your self-talk serves as a regulatory mechanism, which your brain employs to make decisions [1]. Self-talk is an introspective tool, which influences your attitude, behavior, and beliefs [1]. Your brain basically tells itself something to reinforce a belief and instruct your subsequent actions.

Self-talk reinforces your brain's idea of who you are, and thus how you should act [1]. Self-talk makes it easy to determine how you should respond to a situation, because it upholds a sense of how you would normally act that fits neatly into your self-identity. Unfortunately, this can become problematic if your brain is regulating a self-identity that is negative.

The structure of your self-talk is built from your background and becomes a habit because this offers convenience for the brain [2]. If you don't have to think hard about what to say to yourself, your brain can save some serious effort. As your brain thinks a certain thought, it creates a neural pathway [2]. It is likely to follow this same neural pathway every time it encounters a situation that calls for a similar thought or decision. For instance, if you think "I'm an idiot!" when you make a big mistake at work, you tend to think that you're an idiot every single time you make a mistake because that is the easiest neural pathway available to the brain. Forcing yourself to think something more along the lines of, "That was a mistake but I can do better" can create a new (and more positive) neural pathway for your brain to take next time you screw up at work.

Habit change works on two of your brain's built-in decision-making systems, System 1 and System 2 [2]. System 1 is where you rely on old habits to make fast, almost automated decisions. You may beat yourself up for what you do using System 1 but beating yourself does not change System 1's wiring. System 2 is more conscious and deliberate and requires your brain to think hard. When you use System 2, you can make better decisions, which become habitual with repetition [2].

Think about what happens if you are going to a new address for the first time. Your brain saves the route as a neural pathway. This makes it easier for the brain to recall the route in the future. You keep taking that same route every time because your brain knows it. It is easier than forging new neural pathways by taking new routes. But if you keep taking new routes, then your brain gets used to it. With repetition, the pathways for different routes become "saved" in the brain and you can recall all of them when you have to decide which route to take during rush hour to save time.

Your memory works this same way and shapes your self-talk [3]. When you think on a memory, you are actually remembering the last time you thought about it. The same attitudes and feelings you experienced the last time you reflected on this memory will be instantly recalled. This can make you become stuck in a negative loop because you keep revisiting the same negative feelings every time you think back on a memory. You can continue to feel shame and humiliation about that time you puked on someone in high school for the rest of your life, which in turn lowers your self-esteem and mood and reinforces negative self-talk.

The cool thing about memory is that is not static, but rather adaptable [3]. Thinking about the memory in a new way can create a new neural pathway that triggers different feelings. Then, in the future, you have a better response to the memory. For example, when you recall that time your dog died, you naturally reflect on feeling terrible. You may blame yourself. In the future, you can reflect on how you did your best as a dog owner and gave your dog a good life. This makes the memory more bearable every time you think of it in the future, and thus you stop ruminating on how you failed.

Another interesting fact about memory is that your memories are not reliable. They are comprised of splinters of real events, distorted by your brain to fit your idea of reality [3]. Hence, your memories may be reworked to reinforce a negative idea you hold about yourself. Always remember that your memories are not accurate and things are probably not as bad as you are remembering them to be. You can reconstruct a memory as you see fit.

The brain works on a negative feedback loop system [4]. Basically, you have a picture of reality in your brain, which you started constructing as a baby. When your brain encounters situations that differ from this reality, it feels jarred and creates an irresistible urge to act in some way to "correct" the situation to fit into its neat little prepackaged picture. Maybe as a child your parent always told you that you were shy, so now that is your sense of your personal reality. When you are thrust into social situations, your brain thinks, "This isn't right. I'm shy. I'm not supposed to be outgoing in this situation." Thus, it tells you to act shyly in order to fit into its concept of reality. You can perpetuate negative behaviors as a result of this negative feedback system.

Your brain also relies on this negative feedback system to perpetuate your self-talk. When you encounter a situation, the brain tells itself to resort to its usual self-talk to regulate your behavior to match what your brain thinks is consistent for you [4]. Interestingly, serotonin can inhibit this [4]. Since serotonin is a neurochemical generated when you experience something positive, it follows that positive thinking can effectively rewire your brain. So, if you think things that make you happy, your brain starts to inhibit its own negative feedback loop system and rely on a new one that creates even more serotonin.

Changing your self-talk involves forging new neural pathways. This is why it can be difficult, at least at first, to make new self-talk habits. With time, however, your brain will get used to its new neural pathways built on positive thinking and it will start to follow them instead of the old negative routes. It will produce more serotonin which makes you happier as well.

You may have learned negative self-talk in the past. You probably learned it from a parent, who modeled negative self-talk for you, or you learned it from hearing someone criticize you a lot [1]. This formed a neural pathway of negative thinking that your brain takes every single time you have to think about yourself, following its System 1 decision-making loop [2]. It is a habit now. Your memories can also perpetuate negative self-talk as you recall unpleasant feelings and ideas about yourself based on the past [3]. But you can rework that habit and make your brain take a different route when you think about yourself in the future.

One of the best ways to change your thinking is to create self-distance [1]. You can also reprogram your brain by chasing negative thoughts with positive ones. Additionally, you can identify and undermine cognitive distortions that cause you to make poor decisions based on a distorted sense of reality [5]. Doing these two things can create new neural pathways that your brain will follow in the future. This can make positivity habit, thus removing your fallback of negative self-talk. Replacing bad feelings associated with memories can also help you feel better and create a more positive sense of identity that is less painful [3].

You will learn about how to do these things in more detail in Chapter 8, as well as throughout the following chapters.

Chapter 3: Consciously Rule Your Subconscious

Your subconscious is a deeply buried part of your brain, from which System 1 decisions are rapidly generated [2]. Your subconscious drives the thoughts you are consciously aware of. Thus, your self-talk is rooted in your subconscious. To reprogram it, you absolutely must use your conscious to drive home repeated new thoughts to reset the neural pathways that work behind the scenes in your subconscious mind.

Over the years, repeated exposure to negative inputs has created a negative System 1 program [2]. It only makes sense that you are now deeply engrained in negative self-talk. However, you can reprogram your brain with some work. You have to do reprogramming gradually; it does not work overnight. If you have gone through years of negative programming, positive reprogramming can take a while to become habitual. However, this habit is very beneficial because positive self-talk becomes the default for your brain. You will not have to think about it anymore once you reprogram your subconscious to rely on a positive thinking neural pathway.

What Positive Self-Talk Does For Your Brain

You have already learned about what positive self-talk does for your life. But we can go a little deeper by understanding how it affects your brain. Essentially, without going into a lengthy and boring text about neurochemistry, positive self-talk influences your brain's chemistry to make you feel better [6].

Positive self-talk has been linked to an improvement in depression and self-esteem [6]. It all boils down to how you choose to think about stressful events. Now it is true that your self-talk is driven behind the scenes by your negative feedback loop and your System 1 decision-making habits, but you can still make a conscious choice to change those thoughts.

That choice is reflected in your overall mood.

Positive self-talk helps you mitigate the toxic effects of stress from stressful events or situations [6]. As you think through bad things that have happened or are happening to you, you can ease the stress through positive self-talk. This has a wonderful effect on improving your mood and your overall mental health.

It also influences your physical health [6]. Depression and stress can lead to overeating or undereating, muscle aches, insomnia, and oversleeping. If you counter stress with soothing thinking and uplifting self-talk, you can see these symptoms start to vanish.

Positive self-talk also influences your performance. Olympic athletes often use it before a competition to win gold medals [7]. In fact, athletes have trained their brains so well that they can use a simple word to cue a flood of confidence before an event [7]. Dart players noticed higher scores when they practiced positive self-talk before league games [8]. By verbally building yourself up before an event or performance, you can really improve your odds of succeeding.

Furthermore, if you feel happy because you are thinking happier thoughts, you smile more. This makes you instantly more attractive to others [9]. In turn, you have more positive social experiences, which further elevates your self-esteem. It becomes a positive cycle that builds you up more and more.

Beating Negative Self-Talk Out Of Your Head

To effectively reprogram your subconscious, you must consciously think new thoughts. You can achieve reprogramming in a variety of ways, but the true secret is simple: Chase negative self-talk with positive self-talk and use a variety of tricks to induce positive self-talk so that it becomes habit. This can take some time and work, but if you set aside a block of time each day for 66 days to work on your self-talk, it will become a habit [2]. Using positive self-talk is a lifelong activity but it doesn't need to be strenuous, especially as it becomes habitual and automated.

Making a concentrated effort to think positively each day, especially when you encounter stress or negative circumstances, is something you must actively do for the rest of your life. Don't let this overwhelm you. Take it day by day and it will become a part of your normal thinking.

Create Self-Distance

The most constructive part of my self-talk journey was the day when I thought, "What is best for Jeffrey?" I referred to myself in the third person and stepped out of my mind for a moment to ponder what would be ideal for myself. Using an outside perspective, I was able to see what was obvious: I needed to go back to college. I had dropped out for a while and faced a series of setbacks in my career as a result. To further myself, I needed to complete my degree.

Inside my own mind, trapped behind the lens I always used to view my life, I knew completing my degree was necessary, but I kept clouding the idea out with negative self-talk, like "How can you possibly finish now? It costs too much, you don't have the time, and you dropped out before, so why would you finish now?" But when I stepped out of my own mind, I was able to see reality for what it was and make the best decision for myself. I was also able to determine how to reduce the cost of college and fit into my budget, how to make time for classes and studying, and how to motivate myself to stick with it to the end.

Positive self-talk is possible when you step out of the framework that you have erected around your identity. This process is called self-distance [1]. It involves looking at yourself as if through someone else's eyes. This removes the emotional and logical hurdles that you create for yourself based on your limited negative feedback loop system. It also helps you come up with new ideas and creative approaches that can help you overcome hurdles.

To create self-distance, first phrase your self-talk in the third person and call yourself by name [1]. This may feel weird, but that's just because your brain is not used to thinking like this. Ask yourself a series of questions targeted at discovering what is best for yourself:

- What is best for [your name]?
- What would make [your name] happy?
- What would solve his/her problem right now?
- What are the steps to accomplish this?
- What can [your name] do about this today?

When self-doubt or "What if" scenarios rear their heads, think about what someone else might say to those thoughts. For instance, when I thought "I can't afford college," I considered this from a college advisor's position and listed different ways I could. Financial aid, scholarships, and a careful budget immediately came to mind. I then thought "What if I take a loan out and can't get a job and pay the money back?" I reminded myself that people with college degrees make fifty percent more than those who don't to placate this fear.

Visualize

Many Olympic athletes use visualizations to make their goals seem more real to themselves [6]. When you visualize a goal, you can make it seem real to your brain. Then your brain believes that it can achieve success and you feel motivated.

Visualize what you want clearly. Envision how you will feel when you get what you want. Let that visualization motivate you. Whenever you feel discouraged or demoralized, fall back to that visualization to drive you forward.

Set Smart Goals

Part of positive self-talk is thinking in a realistic way that your brain can believe. You can throw positive thoughts at yourself all day long, but if they don't make sense, your brain will outsmart you and resort to negative thoughts that do make sense. Most negative thoughts are rooted in reality, or at least your brain's solid sense of reality. To counter them, you must think in positive ways that also make sense.

One way to make your brain believe what you are thinking is to create a SMART goal, a common mental hack used by athletes [6]. Tell yourself that you can accomplish something and then outline how you can so your brain actually believes you can do it. SMART stands for:

1. Is it specific? You must have a very clear idea of what your goal is in order to accomplish it. A bad

goal is "I want to become a better person" because you don't tell yourself what you really want to do. But a good goal is "I want to raise my income by ten percent to feel like a more accomplished person" or "I want to spend eight hours a week exercising to feel better about myself."

2. Is it measurable? Your goal must be measurable. For example, you want to get ten new contracts in a year. You must determine an actual number so that later you can evaluate your progress and see how close you are to the goal. If you are still far from your goal, you can work harder at it or set up new steps to make it more attainable. Also, you can use measurements to ascertain if your goal is realistic or if you should adjust it to make it more so.

3. Is it actionable? A goal must have specific and realistic actions that you can take to make it reality. You want to list action steps to reach your goal. Breaking goals into smaller steps makes it seem

more possible and less overwhelming.

4. Is it realistic? A goal that is not realistic will fail. Planning to become the richest man in America in one year is probably not realistic. Don't limit yourself but try to think of things that you can actually accomplish using the action steps you determined before.

5. Is it time bound? Your goal needs a deadline so you know when to complete steps to achieve it and you feel motivated to get things done. You might say that you want to acquire four new accounts in the next month at work, for instance. Having that timeline lets you measure the goal and see how many accounts you have acquired in a week, in two weeks, and finally in a month. You can see how close you are to the goal and how much more you must do to reach it by the deadline. Set a deadline for the ultimate goal and a timeline for each action step to make it more achievable. Determine various milestones when you can step back and view your progress.

The Benefits Of Mindfulness Meditation

Mindfulness meditation is an incredible way to master your own mind and reprogram it [10]. Practicing it every day will teach you to focus on things more intently and stop thoughts before they gain any power over you. It is a great way to learn to still negative self-talk and redirect your mind to positive self-talk. The best part about it is that it is a conscious activity, so it helps your conscious mind stay on task and effectively reprogram your subconscious.

Buddha often talked about monkey mind, wherein your mind swings from thought to thought and mood to mood with little rhyme or reason. Negative self-talk and anxiety are often the products of monkey mind. Mindfulness helps you stop the swinging around and the intrusive negative thoughts that tend to come from monkey mind. This can lead to greater peace and inner harmony.

In fact, mindfulness meditation has been found to help patients overcome pain and it has positive implications in the healing of cancer patients [10]. This is because patients learn to focus on their feelings and then control them.

Mindfulness meditation has amazing effects, but it is not hard. Every day set aside five minutes to sit in silence, preferably in a peaceful place with no distractions. Focus on a spot on the wall and determine to look nowhere else. Begin to breathe in through your nose, out through your mouth. Concentrate solely on the act of breathing and looking at the spot on the wall. When you feel the urge to move or look away, resist it.

Intrusive thoughts will begin to cloud your mind. Peacefully acknowledge a thought, then remind yourself to keep looking at the wall and breathing. This will redirect your thinking.

In time, you can increase the increments of time in which you meditate. You can also start to focus on tasks in the same way as you work, clean the house, do the dishes, or perform yard work. Even try it while you are driving and become a much better driver! With practice, mindfulness will become a habit that helps you stay focused and dismiss negative thoughts as they enter your mind.

Start to apply it to your thinking. When you are plagued by negative thoughts, worries, and doubts, you can dismiss those thoughts just as you do in meditation. You can then focus on thinking something more positive. Mindfulness will help you gain the mental control and self-awareness that enables you to do this throughout the day, not just when you are meditating.

Neutralize Cognitive Distortions

Cognitive distortions are forms of negative thinking that distort reality negatively [5]. They can drive you to act in ways that are not helpful to your overall success. Neutralizing them involves writing down your thoughts, determining the applicable cognitive distortion, and then thinking in a new solution-oriented way to that restructures your view of reality and delivers results.

Rooted in cognitive behavioral therapy, this method helps you retrain your thinking over time. You learn to identify and stop poor thinking habits, or cognitive distortions, by replacing them with more helpful thinking. While you can use a therapist to accomplish this, you can also use a journal or workbook (many are available online for free or a small price) and do it yourself.

While there are many forms of cognitive distortions, the most common ones are as follows:

Black And White/All Or Nothing Thinking

This kind of thinking often underlies depression and jadedness. You assume that a person is all good or all bad. You think that by moving, life will become perfect. Then you are surprised and hurt when things don't turn out as black and white as you assumed. Life always has gray areas, a bit of good and bad mixed together. Understand this and you will find your emotions become much more stable.

Generalizations

When you generalize, you lump a person or situation into a broad category. You might generalize that all women are cheaters because one woman cheated on you, or you might assume that a person is bad because he reminds you of your father-in-law. You tend to make life negative when you make these broad generalizations. You may also limit yourself if you make a generalization about a person or job. Determine when you do this and decide to get more information before you make a judgment. Keep in mind that every person and situation is different.

Evaluations

You critique yourself against some sort of pre-determined standards. You may compare yourself to someone else or hold yourself to impossible expectations. You always fall short and this lowers your self-esteem. When you begin to compare yourself and measure yourself, write it down. Determine what you are making the comparison against. Then decide that comparisons are not helpful and you should just accept yourself for who you are and where you are in life. If you want to improve, decide where you can improve and how to do it. Use that determination to drive a SMART goal.

Blaming

You feel the need to assign blame to someone or to yourself for something that has gone wrong. You might accuse someone of messing up your life when you are the one who made a mistake. Or you might blame yourself for someone's death when you had nothing to do it with it at all. Write down thoughts in which you assign blame and then ask yourself what you actually did to cause the event in question, or what someone else did. Decide to focus on a solution instead of dwelling on anger and blaming others or yourself.

Assuming

When you assume, you make a decision that something you don't know is true. You might assume that someone hates you because he shot you a dirty look. You might assume that someone won't go out with you because he or she hasn't responded to your text for an hour. Operating on little information, you assume that something is true and then you act on it. You may be mistaken. It is time to write down the things that you are thinking and determine if there is any basis for your assumption. If you don't have solid evidence for a decision, don't immediately make it.

Catastrophizing

This is where you make a mountain of a molehill. You assume that something is way worse or more disastrous than it really is. This thinking often drives anxiety and panic attacks. Write down something you are worried about. Decide if it really will hurt you as badly as you assume, or if it will turn out badly.

Give Yourself A Pep Talk

Most athletes have success using a self-pep talk to motivate themselves before an event [6]. Pep talks work by convincing your brain that you are able to do something. They build up your energy and self-esteem, creating the perfect recipe for success in your mind.

To give yourself a pep talk, you first must acknowledge the self-doubt that creeps into your thoughts. As you think these thoughts, calmly accept that you feel anxious or doubtful, and then tell yourself, "I want to feel motivated instead." Firmly turn your mind toward positive thoughts that build you up. Let the negative ones have their turn and then redirect your thinking to the motivating thoughts every time.

It is best to emulate someone who has given you encouraging pep talks before. You may think back to a coach, or a parent, or a teacher, or a best friend. Remember how the person spoke and how his or her words made you feel. Focus on that feeling and tell yourself similar encouraging things. You may also find a role model, such as a sports team coach, and watch him or her give a pep talk to learn how to structure yours.

Tell yourself that you can do something. Tell yourself that you have what it takes. And, finally, tell yourself that you will grow from this experience, no matter how you perform. It can be helpful to reflect on victories and triumphs you have had in the past.

Give yourself a pep talk anytime you feel nervous or doubtful about your abilities. You can do this before a job interview, a first date, a speech, or a big performance. You can do this when you're starting something new or taking on a big project that fills you with anxiety. Pep talks are especially helpful before big life events or changes when you feel most vulnerable to insecurities and doubt.

Achieve The Flow State

The flow state is an interesting state of calm deliberation and determination that martial artists, competitive athletes, and CEOs often utilize to get things done [11]. While the flow state leads to increase productivity, its true point is to learn to focus on the present to lead a happier life. Learning to exist in the flow state takes practice, which is optimized by using mindfulness meditation. Once it becomes habit, you will find that you have greater concentration, improved productivity, and better mental control that enables you to stop negative self-talk in its tracks.

When you are in the flow state, you are not letting anything distract you. You don't have room in your mind for insecurities. The results you are aiming for will drive you to work hard and they will boost your confidence.

Achieving the flow state is easiest when you are doing something you love because you are more willing to pour your entire heart into it. But it is more than possible to achieve it when you are taking on a daunting or tedious task. Challenges usually enable you to unlock the flow state.

- First, address your physical state. You must be comfortable. You must not be hungry or tired. Physical discomfort will kill flow, so get comfortable before starting to ensure you don't suffer needless distractions from your own body.

- You must clear all distractions, including intrusive thoughts. Turn off your phone and choose to answer calls and emails at a later time. Make your space quiet so that you aren't distracted by noise. Ask other people to leave you alone.

- Spend a few moments meditating on a specific spot on the wall to clear your mind and gain laser focus. You must only look at that spot, as you breathe in through your nose and out through your mouth. You must treat thoughts and distractions as flies; you see them, you acknowledge them, but you don't chase them. Eventually, they will buzz away.

- Set a timer for 25 minutes. During those 25 minutes, you can only work on one thing. The more time you spend focusing on the task, the more your mind will clear and accept the task as your sole priority right now. You can allow distractions after the 25 minutes is up if you want, but chances are, your mind will become committed to seeing the task through all the way to the end during that time frame.

- Then, turn to your task at hand. Begin working on it and focusing on it. When intrusive thoughts enter your mind, calmly acknowledge them but don't chase them. Always turn your thoughts back to your work at hand. When a physical sensation distracts you, treat it in the same way.

Chapter 4: Self-Talk And Your Family

Thus far, you have learned how self-talk helps you. However, positive self-talk is not just beneficial for your own personal success. It can also lead you to achieve better relationships and better rapport with your family and friends. Your positive attitude and new aptitude for forgiveness can lessen tension. You show your family members more love. They become happier and learn to use positive self-talk from you. In turn, having a more peaceful and happy home life can improve your mood and carry over into other areas of life.

While many people claim to be good at compartmentalizing, the truth is that stress at home tends to negatively impact everything else in your life, from romance to work. You can become less confident if you are at odds with your family, which trickles into your work performance and your social life outside of the home. You also tend to feel stressed and suffer various subsequent physical and mental ailments. Obviously, these things will have a negative impact on the family unit, as well as all other areas of life.

Positive self-talk helps you show your family your good side. It helps you forgive grievances and build better communication to prevent future issues. Furthermore, it can make you feel better, so you are more able to treat your family kindly without taking out stress and unhappiness on them. Being confident and comfortable in your skin helps you overcome insecurities that you may inadvertently take out on your family. This can strengthen your relationships and improve the quality of your love.

Self-Talk To Improve Relationships With Your Family

We all have annoying habits, such as leaving toothpaste uncapped or littering socks across the bedroom floor. When you are trapped in the cycle of negative self-talk, however, you are under greater stress than normal. This can make you less forgiving about small annoyances, which in turn can make you act out aggressively against your family over small things.

Most people have said things they regret to their family members over remarkably trivial things; for example, it is not rare to take a bad day out on your family and explode over something like your spouse leaving the toilet lid up. These explosive and irritable behaviors can create negative feelings and strain between family members, which can cause bigger issues in the long run.

However, if you use positive self-talk, you can start to feel less stressed. That causes you to treat your family with less irritability and frustration. In addition, you should self-talk positively and out loud to your family over small issues, to show them what you are really feeling. They will be more receptive to your messages if you phrase them positively.

For instance, say you come home from a long day and your kids have left the house a total mess. Your normal reaction is to get angry and yell. Yelling only makes your kids feel defensive and even scared of your bad mood. It does not lead to a pleasant evening. Instead of yelling, you say out loud, „I don't like when you leave the house a mess because I step on Legos and it hurts. It is much safer to have a clean house. How about you guys help me pick up?"

As a result, your kids feel more eager to help you clean up. They also learn why you hate messes and why it is good to keep the house tidy. You also feel better because you don't harbor guilt for yelling or annoyance against your family. You don't build up negative emotions that make you cynical. You can simply relax with a tidy house and enjoy dinner with your kids and spouse.

Start by acknowledging when something your family

does annoys you. Look at it objectively using self-distance to see that this issue is not huge. Consider how you feel and how your mood may be influenced by other factors, such as stress at work or a long, exhausting commute. Decide not to take your mood out on your family, and instead let yourself feel grateful that you have a family to come home to. Focus on your feelings of love for your family members, letting it fill your heart and your mind.

When you have shifted into a more positive mood this way, you can think of a solution to the annoyance that triggered you in the first place that is not clouded by annoyance or anger. Think of how to positively word your feelings to your family that does not betray anger or any other bad emotions. Invite them to help you right the issue.

When using positive self-talk to your family, you want to always use positive phrases. You don't want to level accusations at your family members. Instead, say something like, "Let's work on this together." Provide suggestions for what each family member can do to improve the situation. Leave negative accusations and hurtful insults out of the talk.

You should also build communication by clearly stating how you feel. You don't want to do this in an emotional way. For instance, if stepping on a Lego makes you incredibly angry, take some time to neutralize the anger. Then tell your kids in a regular, calm tone that leaving Legos all over the floor makes you angry because it hurts when you step on them. You can then say, „Please pick them up."

Always use „I" messages to communicate what you are experiencing. Then use „we" phrases to help you invite collaboration with your family. For example, maybe your spouse drives you crazy when he or she puts the blender on first thing in the morning while you are trying to wake up. You may normally yell, „I'm trying to sleep!" but now you say, „I love getting my rest in the morning and I feel that I can't do that when you run the blender so early. Could we please run the blender after I get up?" You just used a combination of „I" and „we" messages to effectively communicate your feelings and a solution to the problem.

Finally, don't overload your family members with criticism. This only teaches your family to be critical of themselves and you; it creates a critical environment for everyone in the home and sets a poor model for how you treat each other. Avoid telling your family members about their flaws. Also, avoid saying things like, „You always do this!" or „You never do that!" Always and never are strong words and they are almost always exaggerations.

Never compare your family members to others. You might feel tempted to compare your youngest child, who is temperamental, to his calmer older sister. „I wish you were more like your sister!" This is an extremely critical and hurtful thing to say, as it teaches your child to always compare himself to others. In place of comparison, point out what the family member does that you like to make him or her want to do that more and make you happier. Back to the previous example, you could tell your youngest, „I loved the other night when you didn't throw a tantrum. How about we have another night like that?"

Consider when you want your spouse to do something romantic. You could say, „You never buy me flowers! Rene's husband always buys her flowers," which makes your spouse feel criticized and inadequate and less inclined to do what you want. Alternatively, you could say, „I loved that one time when you brought me flowers. I would love it if you did that more because it makes me feel good." Now your spouse feels praised for something good he or she once did, and he or she wants to do it more to get more praise. You didn't accuse him of anything and you didn't compare him to another person; you simply praised him for an action you want to encourage.

Positive reinforcement generally works better at getting the behavior you want than negative reinforcement [12]. As in the above example, you want to avoid accusations and phrases like always or never. Instead, praise your family member for behavior you like.

How To Avoid Taking Negativity Out On Family

It is common to take the stress of a traffic jam or a long day at work out on your family when you get home. The stress has built up in your over the course of the day, and you can't take it out on anyone at work without getting fired. Your family is an outlet for this stress. Unfortunately, your family deserves your best treatment and your love. Taking stress out on them when they aren't even the source of your stress is a bad way to keep their happiness and loyalty. Many couples get divorced because of this issue.

On your ride home from work, work on calming yourself and diffusing stress. Use mindfulness meditation as you drive to clear your head and focus purely on driving. Play some good music or a great audiobook to put you in an upbeat mood. Throughout the drive, use positive self-talk to also elevate your mood.

Reflect on what you did well during the day. Then praise yourself for that. This can make your day seem less stressful as you relish what you have accomplished. You should also tell yourself, "It was a hard day, but it helped me meet a few goals. I'm proud of myself. Good job!"

Before you pull into your driveway, be sure to reflect on how glad you are to come home. Look forward to seeing your family and relaxing with them. Don't focus on things like how your kids will start demanding your attention the minute you walk through the door or all of the chores you have waiting for you. This only makes you feel stressed before you walk through the door.

List three things you love about your family and three things you are grateful for before you walk through the door. Doing this helps you retain your positive attitude in the face of controversy or annoyance once you are actually around your family.

Maybe these steps don't apply to you because you are a stay-at-home parent or you work from home. Or maybe your stress lies in dealing with other family members who don't live with you and you must neutralize negative feelings before you have dinner with a toxic family member or go help your mother-in-law with a task you don't relish. The steps above can be modified to fit other scenarios. Take time to praise yourself for your hard work and dedication, reflect on things that you love about your family, and take some time to clear your mind of negative thoughts throughout the day or before spending time with family you don't particularly enjoy being around. Focus on the positive rewards of being around your family and how they have made your life better. Don't dwell on the things that you don't like.

If you are a stay-at-home parent, you should also ensure that you take some time to yourself at least once a week. Leave the kids with someone and go do something you enjoy. This preserves your sense of identity and helps you get over the stress of staying at home with the same people, day after day. Be sure to take a few moments out of each day to reflect on good things about your family so that negative feelings and frustration don't build up within you and leak out in your treatment of your family.

Teach Your Children Positive Self-Talk

I grew up in a very critical, negative environment. While my parents are both wonderful people, they tend to be hard on themselves. They also tend to compare and criticize me in a misguided attempt to make me the best version of myself. Growing up in this environment, my subconscious was programmed to be negative. I became an adult who believed that he didn't have the skills to be happy in life. It took a lot of work to overcome this attitude and adopt a healthier one.

The way you use self-talk transfers to your kids [13]. In a study comparing teachers who used positive and negative self-talk on their students, the outcomes showed much better grades and higher rates of self-esteem in students who heard positive self-talk in the classroom [13]. Children model themselves after the adults in their lives. You are a model for behavior to your kids, whether you realize it or not. Your behavior helps them form theirs. By using negative self-talk, you are setting a model for such negativity in your children. They will internalize this and start using negative self-talk themselves.

Many parents think that their bad habits will not transfer to their children as long as they hide these habits. For instance, you may use negative self-talk, but you speak positively to your children. That is great, but your children still see you using negative self-talk on yourself. Thus, they are still learning negative self-talk from you.

Don't let them grow up surrounded by negative thoughts and feelings. Set a better model by talking to yourself positively in front of them. When you make a mistake, tell yourself that you forgive yourself and then reason out a solution to teach them that all problems have solutions and self-forgiveness is possible. When you want to criticize yourself, focus on praising yourself instead to teach them to do the same. When you feel apprehensive or negative about something, speak optimistically out loud to teach them to always have a positive attitude.

By setting such a model for your children, you teach them to grow up and use positive self-talk on themselves. You also expose yourself to positive self-talk, which makes it more of a habit in time.

Always use your self-talk to model the way you talk to your kids. You want to speak to them the same way you want to speak to yourself. Don't compare or criticize them; simply encourage them and praise them for their positive attributes. When they are scared or anxious, uplift them with a pep talk. If you ever hear them speaking negatively, tell them how to rephrase that talk positively.

The way you talk to your spouse also influences how your kids grow up. You want to set a great model by always speaking to your spouse positively. Use constructive feedback instead of criticism, offer your spouse tons of praise, and focus on solutions to conflicts or problems as opposed to dwelling on the unhappiness of bad situations. Your marriage will improve, as will your kids' attitudes and future marriages.

Transfer Positivity To Your Spouse

An essential part of a good marriage is having continually positive interactions with your spouse. As you well know, marriage is not always happy. Stressful times and tense issues will inevitably arise throughout your relationship. However, the difference between couples who stay married and couples who get divorces tend to center around good conflict resolution skills.

Using positive self-talk can help you transfer positivity to your spouse. Your behavior will create a model for how your spouse feels toward you. Therefore, create a positive model. Your spouse will respond in kind.

Speak To Your Spouse Nicely

Creating a good model centers around speaking to yourself kindly. But you should also speak to your spouse kindly. Using the tips in the first section, speak to your spouse in a way that leaves out comparisons, accusations, and insults. Stop exaggerating your spouse's faults and focus on his or her good qualities. Communicate your feelings clearly with "I" messages and follow them up with "we" messages proposing collaborative solutions. Offer your spouse lots of positive reinforcement for behavior you want to encourage and politely ask for him or her to stop behaviors that bother you.

Focus On The Good Things

You should express lots of gratitude to your spouse. Always praise him or her for doing well. Tell him or her how grateful you are to know him or her.

Bringing home thoughtful gifts, even things as small

as your spouse's favorite candy bar or soda, is a great way to express gratitude and love. I like to bring my wife flowers "just because." This makes her feel appreciated and loved. In return, she likes to give me back rubs after a long day of sitting at my desk.

When your marriage hits a rough patch, you can calm the storm by taking time to reflect on the things you love about your spouse and the good parts of your marriage. This can help you stay positive and hopeful. It can motivate you to work through all the problems because the problems are worth the overall happiness you gain from the marriage.

Listen Impersonally

Listening is very imperative to any relationship. Sometimes, you may not want to hear something your spouse has to say. You may be faced with painful conversations. Listen to your spouse, nevertheless, and then take some time to meditate on his or her words.

Acknowledge negative emotions you may feel and then think of how you can feel more positively about the situation. Figure out how you can use the criticism constructively. Using CBT, analyze the situation when you take something personally to see if it is less of a big deal than you are making it out to be. You can always ask your spouse to clarify something or ask if he/she meant something hurtful. Your spouse can help you work through any negative emotions you may have about a conversation.

For example, when my wife claimed that I was being selfish by hogging the remote one night, I felt very hurt. Using my journal, I analyzed the situation and decided that I was probably assuming what she meant and catastrophizing the situation. I later asked her, "Did you mean that I'm a selfish person?" She clarified that she meant I was being selfish at that moment but that I'm a great person and she loves me.

I instantly felt better. We were able to overcome the issue.

Respect Boundaries And Needs

Respect your spouse's needs. There may be times when you infringe on your spouse's boundaries or fail to meet your spouse's expectations. Many people take their spouses' negative feedback far too personally and refuse to work on the issues at hand. This is a good way to alienate your spouse and break down your marriage.

If your wife complains about you making her uncomfortable when you speak to other women, for instance, you can use that to strengthen your relationship by changing your conversation toward other females. Be willing to change for your spouse.

Don't let anger and frustration build up when your spouse asks something of you. Instead, think of how you love your spouse and want to make him or her happy. Self-talk yourself into accepting your spouse's needs and not taking those needs as insults to your ego. Remember why you love him or her to convince yourself that changing yourself is worthwhile. A good marriage is founded upon a willingness to sacrifice certain activities or habits for your spouse's comfort and happiness.

Repel Pessimism

When your spouse is being negative or pessimistic, he or she can really lower your mood and feed your habit of negative self-talk. Always turn this around by responding positively. Teach your spouse to have a good attitude by having one yourself.

Say your spouse is anxious about an upcoming showcase and keeps talking down on herself. You can build her up with a pep talk and make her feel better. She will become happier and that will rub off on you. Essentially, you both create an equilibrium of positive emotions that nourish both of you.

Do Happy Things

Having a life apart from your spouse leads to a healthier relationship, as well. You tend to keep your independence and a sense of being your own person. You also have time away from your spouse, which helps you get over any irritation you may feel over little things. Have a hobby and friends outside of the marriage to blow off steam.

However, this does not mean that you should not spend time with your spouse. Your spouse should always be your number one priority. Becoming so obsessed with your new car that you fail to spend time with your wife is an example of how you can take a life outside of your marriage too far. You want to dedicate time to your spouse each day. Communicate that you love him or her via text message once a day when you are not together.

Doing things together outside of your normal routine can keep you both entertained and happy, as well. You should have mutual friends and activities or hobbies that you both enjoy doing together. Marriage counselors recommend for couples to have "date nights" where they court each other, just like before they got married. Dating can keep the romance alive and prevent your marriage from getting stagnant. A romantic dinner every now and then, a lovely vacation while the kids are in summer camp, and other such activities are good ways to date your spouse.

It is helpful to think of your marriage as a constantly evolving relationship. You must put in work to keep it from evolving into something sour or plain bad. You can keep the love alive through the same work you put in getting your spouse to fall in love with you.

Love at first is usually a trick of the memory [3].

There was actually a lot of work that went into the growth of your love for each other. Hence, always remember that feelings can change and are not permanent. You must continue to put in the same work to get the same results. Make some effort to keep the love alive through dates and your marriage will stay strong and happy.

Eliminate Jealousy And Insecurities

It is also key to build up your own confidence with self-talk. Often, you take things your spouse says too personally because of an insecurity you have that your spouse does not even know about. You may also feel insecure compared to others, so you become jealous and let jealousy fuel fights and distrust. Having confidence helps you overcome this.

For example, I had an insecurity about my lack of muscles for a long time. When my wife even looked at a male model on an ad or a show, I would feel a wave of resentment and jealousy. I was telling myself, "She probably wants someone who looks like that rather than me!" In time, I realized that I was the only one thinking this. I was letting my own insecurities about my body create a lot of strife and conflict with my wife when she loved me exactly for who I was. Therefore, I decided to work on my body satisfaction by going to the gym and repeatedly telling myself that I actually looked good. The result was less jealousy and more happiness with my wife.

With a happy family, you can have a better work life and more success in business. However, there are additional self-talk techniques and tricks to make your business stronger. Read on to learn how to enhance business with positive self-talk.

Chapter 5: Self-Talk For Business Success

What if I told you that you are your own worst enemy? It's not something you want to read, but it's true. Many people talk themselves out of success and happiness. Everyone has inner potential, but some people don't realize their potential due to insecurities or fear that they entertain inside their heads. They pass up on great opportunities and make excuses to avoid taking risks. The result is a life of failed and missed chances, stuck in a rut.

The key to your success really depends on you. By making a choice to take opportunities and live your best life, you make it possible. You can use positive self-talk to overcome fear and doubt. You can motivate yourself with intrinsically positive language.

When was the last time you felt excited about something? What was your thought process? Capture that moment in your mind and really experience it again. From now on, that same feeling is how you want to regard your business and your work life. Feel excited and imagine what could happen. Work to make things true, without letting doubt hold you back.

Make Impossible Tasks Possible

Find Solutions

People often assume that something is impossible. They find a dozen reasons to support this self-defeating belief, and those reasons are probably valid. You might think, "It will take forever to get my degree; I don't have that kind of time or money right now" or "I can't afford to launch my own business." But in reality, these "valid" reasons are just excuses. Instead of viewing these hurdles as challenges to overcome, you dwell on them and let them take control of your life. You give them far more power than they deserve. It is time to take that power back for yourself.

The science of motivation entails making the impossible possible. The very first (and perhaps most paramount) part of motivating yourself is removing the belief that something is impossible. You can do this by viewing all of the reasons why you *can't* accomplish something as simple hurdles to clear [14]. Basically, think of issues that may prevent you from something as a problem to be solved, rather than a wall blocking your progress.

I faced this when I wanted to go back to school. Without my degree, I had hit a dead end in my career. Plus, I really hated my job! Every job I wanted required a degree. I felt that life without a degree was impossible, but I also felt that obtaining my degree was impossible. So, I felt stuck and feeling stuck made me depressed. Then I realized that I was creating barriers around my mind, preventing myself from moving forward. Obviously, I wanted a degree, so what was stopping me?

First, I looked at the financial aspect. No, I didn't have the cash in hand to just pay my tuition and finish. But I knew there were ways to raise the money. I looked into financial aid and loans and made school possible.

Next, I considered the time barrier. Yes, it would take a few years, so I couldn't expect immediate results. And yes, not all of the coursework would be meaningful and fun. But I realized that if I at least did something, then the time commitment would be worth the end result.

Finally, I often used the logic "What if I don't get a job?" to limit myself. I realized that I was stopping myself from finishing college by focusing on a what-if scenario that may not even happen. Statistically, I knew people succeeded more with college degrees and earned more money. I decided to focus on that positive instead of the negative what-if.

Do you see what I did? I identified the biggest hurdles that made me assume something was impossible. Then I looked at them from different perspectives to find creative solutions to each problem. In the end, I was motivated enough to make my dream happen, and it all paid off.

Negative self-talk tells you that you can't do something. Positive self-talk says, "How can I do this?" You don't let anything get in the way. If there is a problem, you tell yourself that you can surmount it and you brainstorm how to go about doing that.

Gather Resources And Allies

Often, you dismiss an idea the minute a hurdle shows up. Now, you must think about the hurdle differently. Do things you never dared before – like asking people before you assume they will tell you no or looking into resources to help you get to where you want to go. You are not alone. Arm yourself with people and resources to make something happen. Research options and find out what is really out there. Never just assume "There is no way."

For example, my niece had some financial issues and her car was repossessed. For years, she couldn't get a loan, so she kept buying cheap cars that were on their last leg and dealing with expensive repairs. One day, she decided to take a different approach and actually talk to a bank and a car dealer to see if her financing options were truly as restricted by her past repossession as she had thought. While many lenders refused to lend to her, she actually managed to find one. Now she has a much safer and more reliable car. By talking to people and learning about her options, she was able to get rid of the assumption that she was stuck driving rattle traps forever.

Self-talk yourself into asking if there are options you have not explored. You probably have overlooked some possible resource or person who could help.

Now, look into how to make something happen. Just by taking this proactive approach, you start to build motivation and a sense that something is possible.

Are Your Barriers Even Real?

Consider if a barrier is truly real. In my case, I was dwelling on a what-if scenario, "What if I can't get a job?" There are always at least two possible outcomes to every scenario, either negative or positive. Choose to focus on the best possible outcome. It may not happen – but it may happen, too. If you don't try, you won't get to see the best possible outcome.

Try to stop catastrophizing possible bad outcomes, as well. You might assume that you will not make much money if you start your own freelance business. Well, is that really a horrible thing? We all know that money is essential to survival but taking a pay cut in exchange for a career that makes you happy is usually not going to end your life. Ask if a possible bad outcome will truly destroy your life or if you can survive it. Chances are, you can survive it, absolutely no problem.

Use Love To Drive Success

In a study, the main difference between students who feel motivated to study for math class and students who don't depends whether or not the student thinks he enjoys math [14]. When you do things you hate, you tend to feel no motivation. But when you do things you love, or at least work toward something you love, then you feel much more inclined to do it.

To make something possible, focus on what you love about your goal. Focus on how it will make you feel good and how it will improve your life. Use these thoughts as a motivational push toward success. You should write them down and post them somewhere you can see every day to keep your resolve strong.

There are two types of goals: mastery and

performance [14]. Mastery goals are when you feel determined to become competent at something. Performance goals are when you want to stack up to others and beat the competition. A study proved that performance goals tend to drive people to perform better on a test than those with mastery goals [14]. Therefore, you may find that setting a performance goal will motivate your success more because you tend to care more about what others think than how well you do at something.

So, if you are sad that you are not doing as well in life as your brother, use that to motivate yourself. You want to stack up or even beat your brother, and thus you do everything you can to accomplish that goal. Supposed character flaws, like competitiveness and sibling rivalry, can actually be very helpful.

Change your negative self-talk in this area. You should quit comparing yourself to others and feeling dismal that you don't stack up, thinking, "Everyone else is better than me!" Instead, you should think, "I want to do as well as this person I know, so I'm going to do it." Be positive when you use comparisons and evaluations.

Use A Mantra

Barriers to success are numerous. It makes you wonder how some people ever become successful. The true trick is to self-talk yourself that you can do anything. Recite the mantra "I can do this" at least three times. You should also recite this mantra whenever you feel like giving up.

Then write down what issues you are facing that block your success. For each issue, think of at least three solutions. Explore all of your options and write them down as well. This will break open so many doors for you.

Improve Your Interpersonal Relations

One day, your boss calls you into his office and berates you for a mistake. You feel horrible and you go home in a depressed mood. You think about how you hate your boss and your job and you want to quit. And you feel that you can't do anything right.

This negative self-talk at play, breaking down the quality of your relationships at work. You let your inner voice get to you, convincing you that everything is horrible and you hate everyone in the office. Your self-esteem suffers even more than it has to about making a human mistake.

You can change your self-talk to build up your relationships and your self-esteem at work. Use positive self-talk to recover from the ego blows that conflicts at work deliver.

Don't Take Things Personally

When your boss berates you at work, he or she is not insulting you as a person. Your boss views you as an employee and values your quality of work. When you goof, his or her reaction is toward your work, not you as a person. This is where personal and professional realms tend to conflict. You feel like a terrible person, but your boss is not saying that. You must make the distinction between personal and professional in your mind with positive self-talk.

Many people view work as a source of ego [15]. They draw pride from successes, and they suffer humiliation from failures. This makes their personal and professional lives overlap in a negative way. Remove the ego from your work. Remember that work is about your performance for a company, not your own personality. You are valued purely on what you bring to the table. Therefore, don't take setbacks or criticism as personal insults. Instead, take them as pointers on how to hone your work to fit the company's needs and become a more valued worker.

You can also stand out to your boss by requesting constructive criticism. Ask him or her, "What can I do better?" He or she will appreciate this rare yet noble bid for self-improvement.

Rely On Yourself

To succeed at work, you must trust that you are capable of succeeding. You must rely on yourself and trust your abilities to get things done. No goal or task can be too big for you.

Look for things you can contribute. Volunteer yourself for activities or tasks you are capable of doing. By showing your confidence to others, you inspire them to have confidence in you. This can raise you to the top of your team.

You should give yourself pep talks. "I can do this." "I

have what it takes." Saying things over and over convinces you that they are true. Then you act accordingly.

Speak Positively To Your Co-Workers

Just like how you can transfer positivity to your spouse to make him or her more positive, you can transfer positivity to your co-workers. Your co-workers will find your positive attitude appealing and will follow suit with their own behavior.

Start by always presenting praise and compliments to your co-workers to make them like you more. Smile more, too. Being pleasant to be around will make you fit in better at work.

You should learn to phrase criticism tactfully. You don't want to tell someone, "You are wrong" or "You are horrible at this!" or "You did the worst job I've ever seen." You want to say something more like, "I can appreciate what you have done, but I see room for improvement." Then offer tangible ways the co-worker can improve.

Don't take bad moods or stress out on your co-workers. Breathe through emotions instead of yelling or snapping at others.

Project a can-do attitude by always inviting others to help you find solutions. You can build up everyone's morale when you encourage everyone to work together to overcome a setback or hurdle. Pep talk yourself and everyone else by saying, "We can do this! We just have to pull together and make it happen!"

Invite Teamwork And Collaboration

You've probably seen those motivational posters, saying lame things like "Teamwork makes the dream work!" But these posters are not wrong. To truly improve the quality of your work relationships, you must inspire a sense of collaboration and cooperation between yourself and everyone else in the office.

Remember in Chapter 4, when I covered inviting collaboration with your family using "we" phrases? This approach to communication is even more essential in the work atmosphere. You want to invite collaboration to fix problems and meet goals with all of your co-workers. An organization is like an ecosystem, where every member contributes something to the overall goal. When one member is left out or not utilized, the whole team suffers from the lack of value that that one person can add to the work being performed. Hence, you must include everyone.

There is always that one person in the office who seems lazy and/or incompetent. Often, these people are simply unmotivated to rise to their potential. Including them in the team can motivate them. In turn, that motives you more. You should find the specific strengths that this person has and assign that person a task that uses those strengths.

When You Don't Like A Co-Worker

Just like you shouldn't take things said at work too personally, you should not base your interactions with your team on personal feelings, such as dislike. This is obviously easier said than done. Some people in the office just don't behave like adults, while others have completely communication styles and work preferences than you which can make working together extremely difficult.

To get over the sense that you don't like someone, focus on the person's positive attributes and strengths. Build the person up in your mind. As you treat this person more positively, his or her treatment of you will likely improve.

Improve communication by changing your style.

People communicate using modalities [16]. One person might process information visually, so he communicates in a visual way, saying things like "Do you see what I see?" or "Picture this!" But his communication is lost on the co-worker who uses an auditory modality and processes auditory information better, and who prefers to say things "Do you hear what I'm saying?" or "Listen to this idea!" The two can find common ground by modifying their modalities. The guy who is more visual would be wise to avoid using graphs and flow charts in a presentation to the lady who uses an auditory modality; the lady with the auditory modality would benefit by communicating to her co-worker using pictures or PowerPoints.

To improve relations with someone who is hard to work with, you should adjust your modality. Miscommunication and annoying mishaps can be avoided thusly. You may think, "Why should I be the one to change? Why doesn't anyone try to adjust their modality for me?" Well, other people have not read this book. You can be the bigger person and make a positive difference at work by taking responsibility for your actions through the knowledge you have obtained in these pages. Your self-esteem will soar when you are the one to trigger positive changes at work.

Realistically, you won't get along with every person and sometimes you will have conflicts with co-workers you normally get along with. It is common to have at least one co-worker who acts like a petulant child and spreads gossip, as well. You can use a stress-diffusing self-talk technique when a co-worker starts to get under your skin.

First, take a quick break, such as a bathroom break. Spend some time sitting in silence. Close your eyes and focus on the in and out of your breathing. Tell yourself, When I open my eyes, I will no longer feel mad. Wait a few moments and then open your eyes. The irritated feeling should vanish. Now go back to work and focus on your task, rather than the person who is angering you. When you start to feel irritated again, redirect your thoughts back to your task at hand to regain concentration on the right thing.

Be Assertive

One of the only ways to get by around people is to use assertive language [17]. Assertive language is not rude or aggressive. It is not passive or manipulative, either. You simply state what you want and stand by it.

Assertively set boundaries at work. Let people know what you expect and what you don't tolerate. Using "I" messages, communicate things in clear terms. Don't let anger or insults seep into your words. Speak levelly and firmly, while holding eye contact. Be sure to be polite and use phrases like "please." After you ask someone to do something, say "Thank you" as if they have already done it. This motivates people to complete what you ask of them without argument.

A lot of issues with your relationships at work can be eradicated by setting boundaries. People know what is wrong – but they like to test boundaries and see what they can get away with. By setting and standing behind your boundaries, you can easily gain the respect of others. You may fear that people will get mad at you, but it is more likely that they will gain healthy respect for you when you stand up for yourself.

Gain Self-Motivation For Tedious Tasks

Every job has its fun, interesting aspects…and it's not-so-fun aspects. The tedious or challenging parts of our jobs may not be fun, but they are part of the day-to-day. You must get used to such tasks and you must learn to get them done if you want to be successful.

Don't assume that every rich CEO spent every day of

his life sipping coffee in front of his awesome view of the city. He was probably once a paper pusher, and later he was in middle management, doing things he hated. Now he is still forced to make hard decisions, endure boring meetings, and handle rejections and losses. You may envy somebody, but never assume that any other person has it all. Everybody has challenges and boring or unpleasant moments at work.

You should pinpoint the parts of your job that you don't like very much. What do you always put off until the last minute? Maybe you are not much of a phone person so you procrastinate phone calls and call in sick for conference calls. Maybe you hate doing paperwork, so you let it accumulate in a big stack until it becomes truly overwhelming. Maybe the act of going through documents with a fine-toothed comb gives you a headache so you dread it until you have no choice but to do it. Write down precisely what you hate about your job and what you tend to procrastinate.

Now, explore the reasons why you hate these particular tasks. What do they make you feel? Are you afraid of failure, or of public speaking? Are you not good at math? These reasons are all challenges to overcome. If you are bad at math, for instance, you can take a refresher course to help you handle the mathematical aspect of your job. Make the reasons you hate certain parts of your work disappear so that you can accomplish them.

Create A System

The most helpful part of motivation is creating a system. Systems are smooth routines that you follow to accomplish certain tasks; they automate the process for your brain. You can start your work day with something you hate, such as paperwork. Get it over with and consider how great you'll feel without a looming stack of papers to fill out at the end of the day. Once the paperwork is over with, you can shift to things you like more about your job.

For instance, I know several social workers. Often, paperwork is the thing they hate most about their otherwise rewarding careers. Most social workers have overcome this hatred by having a system in place to get paperwork done. For five minutes after a meeting with a client, they dedicate themselves to filling out paperwork. If they have to move on to something else, they leave themselves sticky notes for what to finish. Then they finish the paperwork in spare moments before they treat themselves to lunch or a break. They do this to automate the process they hate so much so that they don't procrastinate.

Reward Yourself

Always reward yourself after you complete a task. Doing it right before lunch or a break is a good way to motivate yourself because you know you will enjoy your free time so much more without the looming thought of the task you dread on your mind.

Always tell yourself, "You did a good job!" when you complete an arduous or unpleasant task. Your brain will respond to this message with a flood of feel-good serotonin. In the future, it will feel more motivated because it anticipates that rush of serotonin again. Tell yourself what a good worker you are and how well you did to reward yourself.

Work In The Flow State

Achieving the flow state also helps you with challenging aspects of work. Clear your mind with meditation, reduce distractions, and set a timer for 25 minutes. Then throw yourself into the dreaded task at hand. At the end of 25 minutes, you can move on to something else, but you'll probably want to see the task through to completion.

Break Tasks Down Into Steps

A task seems overwhelming when you view it in its entirety. But when you break it down into bite-sized chunks, your brain sees how it can accomplish the said task. It can then figure out how to tackle the task, bit by bit until it is completed. In fact, studies have indicated that there is increased brain activation and thus better performance when you use subtasks while driving [18].

First, look at the ultimate goal. Then, establish the subtasks that will accomplish that goal. Say your goal is to finish your taxes. You start by gathering documents together, then by signing into your tax account, then by filling out the first page, and so on.

Make a checklist on a piece of paper or in your phone. There are great checklist apps for your phone. Write down the main task and then list subtasks under it. After you complete each subtask, check it off and take a moment to tell yourself, "Great job! Now you're one step closer." This is positive encouragement to keep going until you can check the whole task off. You can also measure your progress, which is essential to every SMART goal. As you see yourself getting closer and closer to completion, you will feel more victorious and motivated to carry on.

Have A Life Outside Of Work

I love what Jennifer Aniston's character in *Office Space* said to the main character: "Lots of people hate their jobs. But they find something that they enjoy." It is true that if you hate your job, you can balance that negativity out with activities that you love outside of work.

Spending too much at work can burn anyone out. You need to get away and stop thinking about work for a while. As you go home, redirect your thoughts to things other than work. Leave work at work, in other words. When you are lying in bed at night and you start ruminating on a project you have to do tomorrow, clear your mind with a quick, silent mindfulness meditation.

Be sure to have a hobby, exercise class, fun club, or something else to do that has nothing to do with work. Spending time around other people and not thinking about work can refresh you and reset your brain for the next workday. You no longer feel as if your life is work because your life contains many other elements.

Does this mean that you should tolerate a job that withers your very soul? Absolutely not. I didn't, and I'm so much happier as a result. If you positively hate everything about your job, take some time to yourself to see if your interest in it renews. If time away doesn't help, then you need to focus on finding a new job. Let the hatred you feel for your job be your motivation to find something better. Tell yourself, "I deserve to be happy" and then coax yourself to abandon fear to find a new job.

Win That Promotion

You work hard for a promotion, and it goes to someone else. You think "Next time" and keep working hard. Then someone else gets the laurels once again. Now, you feel bitter and you think, "My boss just doesn't like me. Good things only happen to other people."

Remember, what you think is what you are. If you take a defeated approach to life, you will be defeated in life. The real success is in believing in yourself and staving off the bitterness that getting passed over can bring.

You can start by self-talking yourself into believing that you are worthy of that promotion. If you believe that a promotion is an attainable goal, then you will be more inclined to work hard to achieve it.

If you get passed over, don't take it as a personal reflection of who you are as a person. Think, "I deserved that but I didn't get it. How can I improve myself to get it next time?"

You should use rejections constructively. That way, you can improve your performance to get the recognition you deserve.

Sometimes, you may be a great worker and a valuable asset to the company, but you don't do anything to get your boss's attention. Of course, you will be passed over if you don't stand out. Often, the people who speak the loudest are the only ones who are heard. To gain attention at work, start to speak up. Let your boss know you want a promotion and why you deserve it. Volunteer ideas out loud and think creatively to stand out from the crowd. Do things a bit differently to get your boss's notice.

When you do something, be sure to point it out to your boss. You may feel embarrassed to promote yourself so blatantly, but the people who get promotions and raises tend to be the biggest self-promoters. American culture does not reward shyness or modesty; letting people know what you have done well is often the only way to gain their admiration and respect. So, the next time you land a huge account, announce it to your boss proudly.

Ask your boss for some time. Then present to him or her your greatest achievements and accomplishments and skills. Point out how you can use them in a new position. You may also point out strengths you have that your current position does not require, to illustrate how you can contribute even more from a new position. Afterward, thank your boss for his or her time. This ingratiates you with your boss by making you look respectful and polite. Urge your boss to think about promoting you before you leave the office.

If your boss tells you no, ask why. Then use his or her words constructively. Perhaps your boss doesn't think you have what it takes. Now you can tell yourself, "Let's prove him/her wrong!" Perhaps your boss thinks that someone else is better suited for the job. Tell yourself, "I will use this competition to prove myself."

In some cases, the cards are not stacked fairly in your favor. Maybe your boss is unprofessional and doesn't like you. Or maybe your boss promotes his family instead of non-family workers. In such a toxic work environment, you may not ever be able to win. You should remind yourself that you are worth more and seek a job that actually values your contributions.

With self-talk at work, you can enjoy much more success. But work and family are not the only areas of life that can benefit from self-talk. Read the next chapter to learn how to begin using self-talk to enrich your social life and make better friends.

Chapter 6: Positive Self-Talk For Social Relations

When I began using positive self-talk, I noticed a huge change in my social life. Not only did I make friends more easily, but my friendships tended to be better quality than before. While I believed that I had good social skills before I started using positive self-talk, I later realized that my negativity was hurting my friendships and attracting the wrong types of people into my life.

Part of my self-talk training included a book entitled *Safe People: How to Find Relationships that are Good and Avoid Those That Aren't.* In this book, I learned that certain people kept me trapped my cycle of negativity and reinforced my toxic beliefs by being negative themselves. I learned to be more discerning about the people I allowed into my life by evaluating if people are safe or not. The book also taught me to believe that I was worthy of safe people.

Self-talk is important for your social life. It makes you more upbeat, which draws more people into your life. It helps you overcome difficulties that hold you back from a rich social life, such as shyness. Finally, it teaches you to believe that you are worthy of good people who treat you well. You are more able to identify toxic people and eliminate them from your life because you know that you deserve better.

As you get to know more people with whom you have quality relationships, your confidence will soar. The fact that people like you will make you like yourself more. You will find more opportunities in life and work. Last but not least, you will have allies to help you through life's trials and tribulations. A good social life is inherent to success, so you should start using self-talk to enhance your social life immediately.

Overcoming Shyness With Self-Talk

Shyness can be the number one thing holding you

back when it comes to your social life. You fail to talk to people, so no one gets to know you. You are forgotten when people throw parties or pick team members because no one really knows you. Dating can be a special kind of nightmare for shy people, as well.

Overcoming shyness is the subject of numerous books and articles. But really, it boils down to one thing: using self-talk to increase your social skills. Since what you think makes who you are, it makes sense that believing you are shy makes you shy. Believing that you are actually outgoing and comfortable around people makes you outgoing and comfortable around people.

Imagine yourself as brave, calm, extroverted, and fearless. Take a few moments to meditate on this feeling. Visualize clearly how you feel in a social situation. The sweaty palms and shakes that you normally feel don't exist in your visualization; you feel totally cool and smooth. Now, imagine what you say to people. Imagine having great conversations and walking out of a party with a stack of business cards from people who really want to get to know you more. Let yourself feel this experience as if it were really happening.

This visualization helps tell your brain what is possible and how to act. But visualizations only go so far. To actually reap the benefits of self-talk for shyness, you need to apply self-talk in real life.

Start by signing up for some social event. It could be a party, or a Meetup, or a networking event. Normally, these events fill you with dread. Using self-talk, repeat the mantra: "I am an outgoing person who will make friends." Focus on how excited you are to meet new people and view this as a chance to make new connections. Remind yourself that your ego does not hinge on what others think of you so that the event becomes less critical and daunting.

During the event, smile and walk tall and straight. Your posture will influence your confidence and the way others see you [20]. Make the first move by going up to people and saying hi, offering a firm handshake. The more people you talk to, the more you will feel outgoing. Be sure to speak in a strong voice at a volume that is ideal for the situation you are in. People will soft voices tend to be overlooked [21]. Several studies have shown that women who speak in louder, deeper voices tend to be taken more seriously and men with deeper, louder voices are more attractive to women [21]. Hence, you want your voice to be fairly deep and loud to make people notice you, whether you are female or male.

Be picky. As you meet new people, evaluate how they treat you and how they treat others. An unsafe person will try to get favors or personal information out of you [19]. They will probably seem very trustworthy and charming, but their motives are likely bad. People who seem warm and caring, who don't ask for personal details, or who appear shy are likely safer people [19]. Listen to your gut on this. Don't pursue relationships with unsafe people.

Doing this helps remove some of the pain that may limit you in social relationships. Chances are, you are used to social rejection and you feel inadequate because of how people treat you. Now, you can dismiss such people as "unsafe" and believe that you are worthy of better treatment [19]. The result is that you walk away from social events with far less stress and misery.

Be sure to analyze your reactions to people. Are you taking what someone said too personally? Are you engaging in comparisons, fueling your jealousy and sense of inadequacy? Are you using black and white thinking, assuming that everyone is all bad or all good? Write down negative thoughts about the social event afterward and see if you are employing any cognitive distortions.

Self-Talk For Better Communication

Before I started doing personal work on myself, I was often nervous about speaking to others. I would stutter as I tried to think of the right thing to say. I would stop talking when people turned and spoke to each other, my thoughts grinding to a screeching halt. And I would talk only about what others wanted because I was scared that starting my own line of conversation would be met with rejection.

In time, I learned that people liked me more when I dominated the conversation and spoke clearly. If I didn't stop speaking and I didn't stutter, people would pay attention. If I told a story or joke, people would listen and even laugh and a whole new conversation would start around the subject of my story or joke. My conversations improved when I started acting like a conversational powerhouse.

One way to achieve this is to speak in front of a mirror. Rehearse a story that you have in mind to generate laughs or open up new topics. Think of interesting facts or current events to bring up. If you speak first and introduce a great conversational topic, people will be more eager to speak with you. Make sure that what you say is positive, however. Complaining will only put people off. But if you praise something, comment on how nice an event is, or give someone a compliment, you can spark a much more engaging and upbeat conversation that other people actually want to take part in with you.

Another way is to visualize yourself as a great speaker. You want to envision yourself possessing eloquence and aplomb. Imagine standing before an audience, delivering a speech to great applause.

Start to practice conversations on strangers in public places. For instance, tell your barista that her hair looks nice and then bring up the latest events in the city as she makes your coffee. Or tell a stranger on the bus a joke. While strangers may not want to talk to you, attempting to initiate conversations with them can teach you how to do so in a more effective manner. You will get more comfortable, especially when you realize that people respond to you positively if you speak to them positively. Plus, the likelihood of seeing this stranger again is slim, so you don't have to worry about being humiliated in front of someone you know.

Now move up to a co-worker you barely speak to or someone you want to get to know. Try to spark a relationship by starting a conversation or offering a compliment. As you see people respond, your confidence will grow yet more.

With this practice, you are readier to take on conversations with people who make you nervous. You also feel more at ease in dense social situations, where you must compete with other people to dominate the conversation and hold someone's attention. The good thing about denser social situations is that you don't have to take it personally when someone stops listening to you in order to listen to someone else. This is just the way of parties and group conversations. Keep inserting yourself in the conversation and be flexible to new topics that others bring up so that you stay relevant in the group. Be sure to speak loudly so people hear you over the din of dozens or hundreds of voices. Keep talking when someone interrupts you to assert your dominance.

Self-Talk To Improve Self-Esteem

Obviously, people value confidence. Having higher self-esteem tends to enhance your success in social situations and that social success enhances your success in life in general. According to numerous studies, most people find confidence very attractive [22].

Perhaps you are not a confident person. Or you are

confident, but you tend to lose your confidence in new situations. While both circumstances are normal, they are certainly problematic.

Start by practicing self-love and self-care. As you love yourself, you tend to feel better about yourself. Working on your cognitive distortions also tends to make you view life in a better light, which increases your confidence. Also, holding a strong, confident posture tends to influence how you feel about yourself and how others perceive you [20].

To build confidence, think back on your greater triumphs. From taking home a blue ribbon at a science fair in the seventh grade to winning a promotion at work, you have undoubtedly accomplished at least a few great things in your life. Always think of them when you feel insecure to remind yourself of how awesome you can be.

Also, recite what you are capable of. Maybe you are

not a very confident person, but one night you were and you did very well at a convention. Think back on that night and how you accomplished that sense of being on top of the world. Tell yourself that since you have done it before, you can certainly do it again. Hold the feeling of your accomplishment in your mind and relish it, letting it fill you. Desire to experience that again.

Before a situation where you normally feel insecure, recite the mantra, "No mountain is too high." Visualize yourself as a tall, strong person who is capable of great feats. Doing these two things reprograms your mind to think of you as a more confident person. As a result, your confidence skyrockets.

After any situation where you were insecure, write down what happened. Why do you feel insecure? Perhaps you embarrassed yourself; remember that most people are more concerned with themselves than you so probably no one even noticed your embarrassment, or they will forget it by tomorrow. Perhaps you felt rebuffed; remind yourself that you are catastrophizing the situation and you were probably not really rebuffed. Try to think of at least three things you did well during the situation that you want to do again, as well.

A large source of insecurity stems from your body image. If you feel fat, unfit, or somehow unattractive, you tend to suffer socially because people can tell that you are insecure. Before any social situation, look at some flattering photos of yourself or look at yourself in the mirror. Tell yourself how beautiful you are and how your body is a miracle. If you still feel insecure, try to dress, fix your hair, or apply makeup in a flattering way to make yourself feel beautiful. Wearing nice clothes (and nice underwear) alone can make you more confident.

Don't search for confirmations of your insecurities in

others. Many people do this as a habit. Perhaps someone makes a fat joke and you take that as a personal insult to your weight; perhaps someone states that he doesn't like women with red hair and you're insecure about being a redhead. Remember that people's opinions have little bearing on your actual life. For each person who doesn't care for how you look, there is probably someone out there who does.

Furthermore, people seldom mean anything personal when they throw out such negative opinions. They are simply negative, judgmental people who make shallow rules about the kinds of people they like based on looks. It is safe to dismiss and ignore these people in favor of people who don't make such comments. Chances are, the person who made a fat joke did not intend for it to hurt you, but he clearly lacks manners. The person who commented on how unsavory redheads are is limiting his social life by basing his choices in women on something as superficial and temporary as hair color. Neither of these people probably meant to attack you personally. They probably did not even know that you harbor insecurities about the things they brought up. They are simply rude, and you should brush their comments off. Refuse to take these opinions as confirmation that something is wrong with you.

If you are still dating, you can apply these tips to asking someone out and making a good impression on a date. But there are a few extra steps that apply to dating. Read on to make your love life amazing.

Chapter 7: Positive Self-Talk For Your Love Life

Your love life can drastically improve as you use self-talk. By building your confidence, you become a more attractive prospect. You also have fewer qualms about asking people out. You are willing to set boundaries and high standards because you know you are worthy of the best. Additionally, you never let shyness hold you back as you go after what you want, always working toward a big end goal.

Ultimately, the same skills you use for your social life will work for your dating life. Playing the dating game is very similar to making new friends. You must project confidence, speak well, and be charming to make a good impression. The goal may be different, but you will be doing many of the same things.

Grow Your Self-Esteem And Improve Your Body Image

Women rate men as more attractive based on their confidence [22]. Men also rate women as more attractive on this scale and continually state that insecure women are turn-offs. Having high self-esteem is essential to handle the rejection and pain that can arise in dating.

Dating can often feel as nerve-wracking as a job interview. You must make a good impression and even then, you still may not stack up to the competition. Therefore, you want to solidify the belief that you are absolutely worthy of winning first place in someone's heart. You must strive to accept yourself for who you are, so that you find the right partner who actually cares for you.

Love at first sight is typically just a trick of the memory [3]. Hence, no one will just love you on the first date. Nor will you fall in love with someone on the first date. Get rid of that idea. The true purpose of a first date is to establish yourself as someone worth getting to know, or in other words, making a good first impression. You can't do this if you talk down on yourself, behave nervously, or speak little because you are ashamed of yourself.

First, you want to look your best. Looking good enhances your confidence, but it also gives the impression that you actually care about yourself. This is a huge plus on any first date. Dress to impress!

Second, self-promote yourself. You don't want to hang back in modesty since modesty never pays out for anyone. Point out what makes you a great person. Mention your accomplishments and some cool things you have done in your lifetime. Talk about your positive attitude.

Third, always speak positively about yourself. Now is not the time to criticize yourself or mention your flaws. As you talk about yourself, use lots of positive words and upbeat language. Point out the good that came out of bad situations to prove that you have a good outlook on life. Seek silver linings in everything. For instance, if your dinner arrives burnt, make light of it and find a silver lining in the fact that you get a free meal out of the situation.

Finally, don't focus on yourself overly much. You want to talk about yourself a little bit to let the other person know who you are. But follow each statement about yourself with a question like, "What about you?" This invites the other person to speak about himself or herself. It helps you deflect attention away from yourself, so you don't dwell on your insecurities. By pouring all of your focus into listening to what the other person says, you can come up with relevant responses that keep the conversation going. Your attention will be very flattering to your date.

Before going on a date or asking someone out, give yourself a pep talk. Remind yourself how great you are. That confidence will show through when you make an impression on someone else. You can then have the self-love to sell yourself by telling this person how much you like him or her and how you can offer a great date.

Nothing repels dates faster than a bitter attitude or an attitude that you are not worthy. Think that you are worthy of the best. Don't let your thoughts drift to past rejections or bad dates or your ex; redirect them to the present when they do. When you talk to your new date, don't bring these things up. Focus on the positives in your life to lighten the mood.

Get Someone's Attention

Having more confidence helps you get someone's attention. This is because you fearlessly promote yourself and demand his or her notice. You won't get passed over or rejected as much if you actually put yourself out there and make your crush notice you.

Move elegantly. Walk with a confident posture and try to make yourself taller with a straight spine or even taller shoes. The result is that people notice you more. Don't cross your legs or arms, sit turned away from someone, or point toward an exit, as these things can subconsciously close yourself off to someone. Instead, face him or her head-on and keep your body language open.

Also, wear red. Red tends to be the color of sex [23]. Even just a dash of red, such as red lipstick or a red flower in your hair or a red tie, can make the opposite sex notice you more.

When you speak, speak eloquently. Enunciate clearly and speak in a volume everyone can hear. Propose a conversational topic to initiate communication. Then stimulate flow by listening well and replying to a person's words with a relevant topic. Balance listening with talking, devoting about fifty percent of your conversation to each.

The ideal way to get someone's attention is to stand out from the crowd. You can accomplish this by observing someone and learning what he or she likes. Say you have noticed a girl in your favorite coffee joint, always sipping on the same kind of latte. The next time you see her, smile and offer to buy her the latte she likes. This will certainly make her notice you.

Commenting on what someone is wearing and pointing out similarities can also help you gain attention by stimulating a friendship-based neural response [24]. Say a guy is wearing a Dolphins jersey and you grew up in Miami. You can get his attention by telling him that you're a Dolphin yourself or that you went to a game once. Or say a girl is reading a book you read once. Say, "Good book! I love [insert author's name]." Doing this creates a point of common interest that instantly stimulates someone's dopamine receptors, causing him or her to feel good and want to talk to you more [24].

A final great way to come up with a fantastic opener. This could be a corny pickup line to make someone chuckle. Or you could tell a joke. This approach is risky because someone may not respond to your opener well. But you know that you need to take risks to make life happen. Therefore, come up with some clever attention-getting openers. Your goal is to make someone aware of your existence. Saying something unusual (but not terrifying) will accomplish this goal. From there, you have the person's attention long enough to make a good impression and possibly get a date.

Tell yourself that you can accomplish all of this. Rehearse it in front of a mirror. Visualize how your date will go and emphasize positivity in the visualization. These steps will help you calm your nerves and act more becomingly during the date.

Gain practice by talking to people toward whom you feel neutral. Polishing your social skills with practice can make you more confident when it comes to talking to a person you like, which obviously tends to make you more nervous.

Also, don't blow the situation up in your mind to be bigger than it is. Humans tend to put the people they like on a pedestal and then base their ego on whether or not those people like them back. You can lessen the anxiety that comes with talking to people you find attractive by downplaying the situation in your mind. Tell yourself that this is just a conversation with a potential friend, not a potential spouse. Tell yourself, "If this person doesn't want to be with me, that's not a reflection of who I am. It is a reflection of who they are and where they are in life. I can find someone else who is ready for me." If you do get rejected, repeat this as a mantra to lessen the hurt. Think, "His/her loss."

Chapter 8: Growing Positive Self-Talk As A Habit

In Chapter 2, I talked about how self-talk works and in Chapter 3, I talked about how you can attain it by reprogramming your subconscious with your conscious. While I covered several techniques in that chapter that can help you gain control over your own mind and reprogram your subconscious, I want to touch on a few more now that you can use every day to make positive self-talk a habit. These simple steps can be combined with Chapter 3 to increase your positive self-talk use and eliminate negative self-talk.

Remember, negative self-talk is a habit that you can work to replace with the habit of positive self-talk. Through time and effort, you can change your whole way of thinking. Don't fall into the trap of believing that you can't control your own mind and change your habits just because you have been trapped in the cycle of negative thinking your whole life, you were raised in a negative environment, and/or you have been through some incredibly bad things in life. If I could do it, then so can you. I was raised around negativity and engaged in negative self-talk for most of my adult life, before acquiring positive self-talk through great introspection and personal work. I know that you can do it and see amazing results throughout your entire life.

But you can't wait. You must start today and begin to dedicate yourself to this work. As it takes time to make positive self-talk a habit, you must start sooner than later so that you can achieve your desired results sooner than later.

Power Of Positive Affirmations

Positive affirmations work stunningly well in cementing habits [24]. By repeating an affirmation to yourself over and over, you tend to make your mind believe it. Your mind will think of your positive affirmation automatically whenever you encounter an applicable situation simply because you have created neural pathways within the brain for the affirmation.

Positive affirmations are short phrases that trigger a helpful or positive feeling and image within your mind. By saying an easy-to-remember phrase or even a single word that means a lot to you, you can overcome many things. You can breed such desirable traits within yourself as positive thinking, optimism, confidence, problem-solving, self-efficacy, and gratitude. All of these traits will make you feel better about yourself and about your life.

You want to repeat your positive affirmation at least three times a day. You should also repeat them when you are facing a situation that tests your confidence or patience. The affirmation will only work if you use it. Cement it by using it throughout the day, and then gain from it by using it in trying circumstances when you really need a boost in confidence or positivity.

A good positive affirmation is something that you

identify with. You can think of your own, or you can try one that therapists recommend. Here are a few examples of great positive affirmations to repeat to yourself throughout the day.

- "I know and accept myself."
- "I believe that I can do this."
- "I trust my gut."
- "I have everything it takes to get this done."
- "I will see this through to the end."
- "I always persevere."
- "I forgive myself for my mistakes because I'm human."
- "I am good enough and worthy of the best."
- "I learn from my mistakes."
- "I know I can accomplish anything I set my mind to."
- "I am strong."
- "I live each day to the fullest."
- "I make the best of every situation."
- "I am stronger because of my past." (This one is especially useful if you start to dwell on bad

things that have happened in the past.)
- "I have control over my thoughts, feelings, and decisions."
- "I accept the things I cannot change."
- "I accept others for who they are." (This can be useful when dealing with a toxic or trying person.)
- "I can get through this!"
- "I know what I need to do."
- "I can make a difference."
- "I am beautiful and unique."
- "I try to be the best I can be."
- "I will give this my all."
- "I will make this work."
- "I will continue living, no matter what!"
- "I value myself and my life."
- "I love myself."
- "I love everyone in my life for who they are."
- "I have the patience to accept what I cannot change and the courage to change what I am able to."
- "I'm the best person for this [task, position,

date, etc.]."
- "I am open-minded."
- "This will not get the best of me."
- "This is only temporary."
- "This is my life, my rules." (This one is ideal when someone tries to infringe on your boundaries or make a decision for you.)

Eliminate Procrastination

Procrastination is what you do when you lack motivation or confidence to tackle something. You anticipate its unpleasantness, so you try to sweep it under the rug. One thing I found helpful for procrastination is to repeat "Carpe diem!" to myself. Latin for "Seize the day," this phrase is a great mantra to have when you are battling procrastination.

Focus On The Problems Procrastination Creates

I also like to focus on why procrastination actually creates more problems for me in the long run. For instance, if I put off paperwork for too long, it will accumulate and become even more of an arduous task. Getting it done now will make things easier for me.

Realize that procrastination will only make you miss a deadline. Use the impending fear of hearing anger from your boss or even losing your job if you don't get something done as motivation.

Focus On The Positive

Another helpful way to think about procrastination is to focus on the reward awaiting you when you get something done. Imagine the confidence and accomplishment you feel. Now you are free to move on to more enjoyable tasks, without the threat of the tasks you are putting off looming over your mind. Furthermore, you can finish your work for the day, feeling satisfied. You can go home and not worry about what you have put off.

Always give yourself a reward to look forward to. Once you complete the task you were putting off, treat yourself with a favorite activity. This reward should be substantial enough to motivate you. A massage, a day of golf, your favorite dessert – these are all good motivators.

Remove the element of dread from the equation. You probably put something off because you don't want to do it. You hate the task or feel that you don't have the strengths to complete it. But if you focus on the positives of the task, then you will hate it less. Think about what good it will do you or the good things that may arise while you perform the task. Talk to yourself positively about your tasks. "This is a good thing to be doing right now," is a good positive affirmation for this situation.

Often, if you hate something, you like to say so. You say so to yourself and out loud. All of your co-workers and friends know how much you hate certain things. But you can restructure this thinking by speaking about it positively. When you want to say, "I hate doing dishes!" say "I love dishes!" instead. It may feel cheesy and fake at first, but your words will make a difference in your mind's perception of the task. Then you will feel more motivated to get started.

Treat It As A Step

The task you put off is probably just a small step toward a bigger goal. Perhaps your goal is to recruit ten new clients, but you hate making phone calls. Consider phone calls a small but essential step in achieving the ultimate goal.

When you focus on the goal your task is a part of, you tend to see the purpose of the task. Your brain regards it as important. Therefore, you don't want to put it off.

Your ultimate goal is also a viable distraction. Instead of treating this task as a huge insurmountable challenge, you feel distracted by the knowledge that it is just a part of a bigger picture. You shrink your mind's catastrophic magnification of the task so that you feel less horrible about it, and you become more devoted to the overall goal. The pay-off of the work will also appear like a reward to motivate you even more.

Repeat, Repeat, Repeat

Consistency is key in self-talk. In his book *The Psychology of Influence and Persuasion,* Robert Cialdini talks about influencing people with commitment and consistency [26]. The fact of the matter is, you can influence yourself with this same principle of influence.

To influence yourself, you must understand the concepts at work behind commitment and consistency. When you commit to something, your brain becomes partial to it. Your brain is likely to stay consistent and follow something through. Therefore, consistent repetitions of positive self-talk can make your brain commit to positive self-talk, and in turn, it chooses to stick to that habit throughout your life.

Repeating positive self-talk every day needs to start as a conscious practice. Your habit lies in negative self-talk, so you will have to focus on adjusting that habit to change your brain's commitment. Every time you talk to yourself negatively, create new neural pathways by chasing those thoughts with positive ones. The more you do this, the more your brain will follow the positive self-talk track without even bothering with negative self-talk.

For at least 66 days, make a time commitment to this self-work. Sit down with your CBT journal for at least five minutes at the same time each day and analyze the paths your thoughts take, the feelings these thoughts trigger, and what beliefs underlie the thoughts. That way, you can teach yourself new ways of thinking that are far more helpful. After 66 days, this will become such a habit that you may not need to work in your journal every day. You will simply adopt the positive thoughts as a habit and avoid the cognitive distortions that keep you trapped in misery.

You should also repeat positive affirmations to yourself. This drives the ideas you want to keep home. Three times a day is a good way to start using positive affirmations habitually.

Consistently practice in pep talks when you start to feel down. Take some time to tell yourself how great you are and how much you can accomplish. As you inspire your belief in yourself and your confidence, it will get easier to overcome fear and doubt.

Consistently strive to be positive, no matter the situation. As you start to dwell on how terrible something is, remind yourself to focus on the silver lining.

Every single day, think of three things you like about yourself. Also, think of three things you are grateful for in your life. This is a great way to reflect back on your day as you lie down to go to sleep or as you drive to work in the morning, feeling overwhelmed, apprehensive, or lazy. With time, this too will become a habit. You will learn to appreciate yourself and your life more.

It is essential to be consistent in positive self-talk. When you make it a habit, you will do it subconsciously, and positive things will happen automatically. To automate the process, make a commitment to positive self-talk and practice it every day until it becomes a part of your brain.

Conclusion

Negative self-talk is one of the worst habits that human beings engage in. Unfortunately, your environment, background, and self-beliefs drive this habit. Your mind sticks to negative thinking because that is the easiest thing for it to do. Changing can take some time and work, but it is absolutely worth it.

When you evict the cruel critic in your mind, you open up your life for new and great things. You stop letting yourself drown in fear and insecurity. Your renewed motivation and confidence will fuel vigor for life. As a result, your problems resolve and you have a better work, social, and family life.

Contrary to what many people think, life and other people are not out to get you. The real culprit to your misery, depression, and personal problems is your problematic thinking. Using techniques to reprogram your subconscious, you can essentially reroute your thinking and become a much happier person. The power lies within you to have anything you want. You just have to break down the barriers and rules that your negative thinking erects around you.

Using positive self-talk involves a lot of repetition to reprogram your subconscious mind. You can also use mindfulness meditation to strengthen your mental mastery. Pep talks before a big event or performance can motivate you. Unlocking the flow state is essential for getting work done really well and achieving total concentration and dedication to a task.

As you use these techniques, you start to achieve a habit of positive thinking. While it takes time to perform this programming and build a new, healthy habit, the work is certainly worthwhile. The rewards you receive in the end are priceless.

You should always use positive self-talk on your family. It will foster a more positive home environment. As you teach your kids positive thinking, you will feel like a better parent. You will also be a better spouse as you talk to your husband or wife kindlier.

Positive self-talk is a secret known by many successful people in business. They often engage in positive self-talk without even knowing it; positive self-talk is simply a habit that they are used to. These people do experience fear and doubt, just like any other person, but they use positive thinking to overcome these difficulties. By improving your self-talk, you can make your work environment and performance better, so that you can get those raises or promotions you have been yearning for. You can also find the motivation to get through daunting or tedious tasks. You can unlock the confidence to venture out and start your own business or make a bold career move.

Positive self-talk also grows your social circle. As you

begin to project positivity, more people will enjoy being around. Cue more dates and more friends! You can even overcome shyness by talking yourself up.

The basic key to positive self-talk is talking to yourself like you would a dear friend. Build yourself up and encourage yourself in all areas of life. You deserve to be happy. So, stop letting your negative thinking chip away at your joy, and instead love yourself!

References

[1] Kross, Ethan, et al. *Self-Talk as a Regulatory Mechanism: How You Do It Matters*. Journal of Personality and Social Psychology. American Psychological Association. 2014. Vol. 106, No. 2, 304–324. DOI:10.1037/a0035173

[2] Gardner, Benjamin, et al. *Making Health Habitual*. British Journal of General Practice. 2012. Vol 62, No 605, pp. 664-666.

[3] Bridge, DJ, & Paller, Ken. *Neural Correlates of Reactivation and Retrieval-Induced Distortion*. Northwesten Medicine. Journal of Neuroscience. Vol 32, Issue 35, pp. 12144-12151. DOI: https://DOI.org/10.1523/JNEUROSCI.1378-12.2012.

[4] Williams, Paul, et al. *Serotonin Disinhibits a Caenorhabditis elegans Sensory Neuron by Suppressing Ca^{2+}-Dependent Negative Feedback*.

Journal of Neuroscience. 21 February 2018. Vol. 38, Issue 8, pp. 2069-2080. DOI: https://DOI.org/10.1523/JNEUROSCI.1908-17.2018

[5] Wolf, Alex. *Cognitive Behavioral Therapy: An Effective Practical Guide for Rewiring Your Brain and Regaining Control over Anxiety, Phobias, and Depression.* ISBN13: 9781726691222.

[6] Goodhart, D. *Some psychological effects associated with positive and negative thinking about stressful event outcomes: was Pollyanna right?* Journal of Personal Social Psychology. Vol 48, Issue 1, pp. 216-232. DOI: https://www.ncbi.nlm.nih.gov/pubmed/3981389.

[7] Gregoire, Carolyn. *The Brain-Training Secrets of Olympic Athletes.* Huffington Post. https://www.huffpost.com/entry/mind-hacks-from-olympic-a_n_4747755.

[8] Raalte, JV. Et al. *Cork! The Effects of Positive and Negative Self-Talk on Dart Throwing Performance.* Journal of Sport Behavior. 1995. Vol 18, Issue 1.

[9] O'Doherty, J., et al. *Beauty of a Smile: The Role of the Medial Orbitofrontal Cortex in Facial Attractiveness.* Neuropsychologica. 2003. Vol. 41, pp. 147-155. https://pure.mpg.de/rest/items/item_2614428/component/file_2623264/content

[10] Brown, Kirk, et al. *Mindfulness: Theoretical Foundations and Evidence for Its Salutary Effects.* Psychological Inquiry. 2007. Pp. 211-237. https://DOI.org/10.1080/10478400701598298.

[11] Csikszentmihalyi, Mihaly. *Flow: The Psychology of Optimal Experience.* 2009. Harper Collins. ASIN: B000W94FE6.

[12] Farber, P. D., Khavari, K. A., & Douglass, F. M. (1980). *A factor analytic study of reasons for drinking: Empirical validation of positive and negative reinforcement dimensions.* JOURNAL OF CONSULTING AND CLINICAL PSYCHOLOGY, *48*(6), 780-781. http://dx.DOI.org/10.1037/0022-006X.48.6.780

[13] Burnett, Paul. *Children's Self-Talk and Significant Others' Positive and Negative Statements.* Educational Psychology. 1996. Vol 6, Issue 1. https://DOI.org/10.1080/0144341960160105

[14] Murayama, Kou. *The Science of Motivation.* American Psychological Association. 2018. https://www.apa.org/science/about/psa/2018/06/motivation.

[15] Pierce, Jon & Gardner, Donald. *Self-Esteem*

within the Organizational Context. Journal of Management. 2004. Vol 30, Issue 591. DOI: 10.1016/j.jm.2003.10.001

[16] Conway, Jerome. *Multiple-Sensory Modality Communication and the Problem of Sign Types.* AV Communication. Vol 15, Issue 4, pp. 371-383. https://www.jstor.org/stable/30217403.

[17] Newton, Claire. *The Five Conversation Skills.* Web. N.d. http://www.clairenewton.co.za/my-articles/the-five-communication-styles.html.

[18] Choi, M. *Increase in brain activation due to sub-tasks during driving: fMRI study using new MR-compatible driving simulator.* Journal of Physiological Anthropology. 2017. Vol 36, Issue 11. DOI: 10.1186/s40101-017-0128-8

[19] Cloud, Henry & Townsend, John. *Safe People:*

How to Find Relationships that are Good for You and Avoid Those That Aren't. 2016. Zondervan Publishing. ISBN-13: 978-0310345794.

[20] Carney, DR., Cuddy, A., & Yap, A. (2010). *Power Posing: Brief Nonverbal Displays Affect Neuroendocrine Levels and Risk Tolerance.* Psychological Science, Vol 1-6, DOI: 10.1177/0956797610383437

[21] Ko, Sei, et al. *The Sound of Power: Conveying and Detecting Hierarchical Rank Through Voice.* 2014. Psychological Science. ttps://DOI.org/10.1177/0956797614553009.

[22] Chapman University. New Research on Attractiveness and Mating. ScienceDaily. https://www.sciencedaily.com/releases/2015/09/15 0916162912.htm.

[23] Elliot, A. J., Tracy, J. L., Pazda, A. D., & Beall, A. T. (in press). *Red enhances women's attractiveness to men: First evidence suggesting universality.* Journal of Experimental Social

Psychology.

[24] Carolyn Parkinson, Adam M. Kleinbaum, & Thalia Wheatley. *Similar neural responses predict friendship.* Journal of Nature Communications, Vol 9, Article # 332. 2018.

[25] Cascio, Christopher, et al. *Self-affirmation activates brain systems associated with self-related processing and reward and is reinforced by future orientation.* 2015. Social Cognition Affect Neuroscience. Vol 11, issue 4, pp. 621-629. DOI: 10.1093/scan/nsv136.

[26] Cialdini, R. (2008). *Influence: The Psychology of Persuasion, 5th Ed.* Allyn and Bacon. ISBN-13: 978-0061241895

Disclaimer

The information contained in this book and its components, is meant to serve as a comprehensive collection of strategies that the author of this book has done research about. Summaries, strategies, tips and tricks are only recommendations by the author, and reading this book will not guarantee that one's results will exactly mirror the author's results.

The author of this book has made all reasonable efforts to provide current and accurate information for the readers of this book. The author and its associates will not be held liable for any unintentional errors or omissions that may be found.

The material in the book may include information by third parties. Third party materials comprise of opinions expressed by their owners. As such, the author of this book does not assume responsibility or liability for any third party material or opinions.

The publication of third party material does not constitute the author's guarantee of any information, products, services, or opinions contained within third party material. Use of third party material does not guarantee that your results will mirror our results. Publication of such third party material is simply a recommendation and expression of the author's own opinion of that material.

Whether because of the progression of the Internet, or the unforeseen changes in company policy and editorial submission guidelines, what is stated as fact at the time of this writing may become outdated or inapplicable later.

This book is copyright ©2019 by **Stuart Wallace** with all rights reserved. It is illegal to redistribute, copy, or create derivative works from this book whole or in parts. No parts of this report may be reproduced or transmitted in any forms whatsoever without the written expressed and signed permission from the author.

Printed in Great Britain
by Amazon